The Twist in a Twining Vine

Poems by Bryony Carr and Others

First published in 2011 by Pomegranate Books

© 2011 Bryony Carr

Printed and bound in the UK
by the MPG Books Group, Bodmin and King's Lynn

All rights reserved

No part of this publication may be reproduced,
stored in a retrieval system, or transmitted, in
any form or by any means, electronic, mechanical
photocopying, recording or otherwise, without the
prior permission of the publisher and copyright

ISBN 978-1-84289-014-1

Published by Pomegranate Books, Bristol
www.pomegranatebooks.co.uk

Acknowledgements

I'd like to say thank you to all my friends and my family who have supported me through difficult times, and to everyone who has contributed towards the publishing of this book.

Special thanks go to Thomas Green whose photo of me appears on the dust jacket. Thomas has had a brain tumour like myself and has similar disabilities.

Since I had my first book 'The Race for Life' published in 2004, I have met my soul mate Paul, and hopefully we will spend the rest of our lives together.

I dedicate this book to my dear friend Jamie Buckfield who sadly passed away in 2007 after losing his long battle against an aggressive brain tumour.

Jamie was a brave young man who tackled everything he faced with immense courage. He gave me all his love and hope to go forward and enjoy my life to the full.

I also dedicate this book to all those people and their families whose lives have been affected by a brain tumour.

Bryony Carr

Preface

In April 1996 I was diagnosed with a brain tumour. This was to be the beginning of fifteen years of sickness and uncertainty. It all started just three weeks before my 18th birthday. The brain tumour was a childhood tumour, medulloblastoma, most commonly affecting children aged three to eight and is more prevalent in boys. I was seventeen and female. I will always remember my first thoughts. Questions but no answers.

"Why me? "

"Why do bad things happen to good people?"

"What have I done to deserve this?"

The day following my diagnosis I underwent a ten-hour operation to remove the tumour, waking up to a world of frustration and anger. I couldn't walk, talk or feed myself, communication with the big wide world had ceased, with the added factor of not knowing how long all this would last, if not forever.

Thankfully, the surgery was successful. Afterwards, I had a course of intensive radiotherapy, daily for seven weeks, followed by physiotherapy over the next two years. This was to help me deal with unsteadiness and other co-ordination problems. The tumour had been growing in my cerebellum, the area of the brain that controls the co-ordination of muscles, balance and posture.

The next few years were concerned with getting my life back

to normal and starting to do things that any normal eighteen year old would do. In 1998, I started a degree in Biomedical Sciences at the University of the West of England. At this time I was having regular MRI scans of my brain and spine. During my first year at university the tumour recurred. This time my medical treatment involved chemotherapy and a stem cell transplant.

Now in 2011 I am alive but will be having medical treatment for the rest of my life. Having this kind of cancer has its consequences. The tumour has affected the control over the right side of my body, so I have had to learn to write with my left hand. I also had to give up my dreams of becoming a professional musician and many activities I loved, skiing, dancing and cycling.

In 2005 I was diagnosed with epilepsy. This proved to be more complicated than I expected. More medication to be added to the list! As a result of the epilepsy my memory has been badly affected. But you can learn to cope with things that you cannot control. It's my mobile phone that does the work for me. It reminds me when to take my medication. It seems like the alarm is constantly ringing, loud and proud! A diary also comes in handy.

In 2008, my oncologist Stephen Lowis wrote to my GP, "Bryony is almost the only patient in the UK who has survived a recurrence of medulloblastoma with metastatic disease. This in itself is truly remarkable ."

I do consider myself to be very lucky. Having cancer so early in life has changed me. I sense myself to be a different person now from before, less selfish, more caring and understanding the needs of others. An experience like this has made me appreciate what I have got very much more. My family and friends are so incredibly important to me. I also consider people's feelings more when making decisions on matters that might affect them.

My outlook on life has changed. I don't take things for granted anymore. All I really know is that you should make the most out of life. Try to do what you want despite any hurdles that you may encounter and most of all try to be happy and enjoy the time that you have in this world, whether it be six months or sixty years. The one thing we can say with certainty is we simply don't know. Surviving cancer has left me with many disabilities but these problems haven't stopped me from doing the things I want and need to do.

'The Twist In A Twining Vine' is the second poetry book I have published after my first book, 'The Race For Life'. Poems can reveal so much that words cannot say. I hope that reading this book will give you some insight into the world of fighting to survive and how it is seen through the eyes of a patient and those close to them.

Poems

Professor Anthony Oakhill	15
Upon My Shoulder	16
My Special Friend	17
B.R.Y.O.N.Y.	18
My Valentine	19
The Big Puzzle	20
Youth Cancer Trust	21
Destiny Verses Fate	22
Not Believing	23
Someone Invisible	24
A Spicy Breeze	25
A Hard Game To Play	26
Breaking Free	27
Darkness	28
Tracy Ann House	29
Being Invisible	30
Slipping Away	31
Yearly Curing Troubles	32
Robert Wakeham	33
Mr. Sood	34
Sally Le Masurier	35
Imagination	36
Answers To Questions	37
A Boy	38
Normality	39

Hanging On	40
Four Become Two	41
Religion And Signals	42
My Love For Your Life	43
An Ode To Love	44
Jamie's Death	45
I Do	46
My Brain's Eyes	47
Jamie	48
It's Heaven And My Haven	49
Detached	50
A Beautiful Portrait	51
In The Mirror	52
Words That Speak	53
20 Special Songs	54
Tainted Love	56
30, Young Or Old?	57
My Unwanted Dream	58
Brenda, Jim and Georgina	59
Numbers	60
A Perfect Day	61
A Lady With A True Smile	62
Rhyme Verses Time	63
Living Three Lives	64

The Twist in a Twining Vine

Professor Tony Oakhill

A man full of love for life
Noble in his presence
Thanking him for all
His help and support
Once upon a time I thought life would be quite simple
Now, I know different
You can sink or swim in this world today

Only life is not always that easy
A hurdle in the way which needs to be crossed
Keen to always be positive
He creates an atmosphere of immense hope and trust
I believe that
Life is like a roller-coaster
Looking up, down and all around

Bryony Carr, November 2004

Upon My Shoulder

Upon my shoulder I'll wear this crest,
Which was given to me by the best,
When I look at it I'll be reminded of she,
And remember her loving and support she has given me,
I first met this lady by serving her supper,
Of which was made by a funny looking man called Roger,
Every time I see her she gives me a gift,
And the last one really gave me a lift,
The gift gave me an inspiration to write this poem to give her a cheer,
But I beg you not to pay me a tear,
When my moral gets low my mind goes far away to a happier place,
And I want you to know that next to me there is always a space.

                                        Jamie Buckfield, February 2005

My Special Friend

Jamie Buckfield is
A person you could love forever
My brave and loyal friend
In his young life he has
Experienced more than one would expect

Beginning a period of the
Unknown
Cancer is a word of the unknown
Keeping positive and
Full of hope
In a situation where there is no answer
Every breath that he takes contains his
Love for life and his
Devotion to his family and friends

                                          Bryony Carr, January 2005

B.R.Y.O.N.Y.

Blessed with a heart of gold
Realistic with no fake loving or kindness
Young and full of inspiration
Ongoing and never giving up
Non-stop care, love and happiness
Yes will always be the answer for a favour

All the above are in her name
Imagine what is in her soul

                                        Jamie Buckfield, May 2005

My Valentine

Every day I long to hear her speak
Every day I place a kiss on her cheek

Every week I am blessed with her love
Every week she shines on me from above

Every month, so sweet, so beautiful
Every month she sits like a queen on her throne

Every year the love spills from the hearts of both hers and mine
Every year she is my valentine

                                                Jamie Buckfield, June 2005

To Bryony with great love from J.D. Buckfield

The Big Puzzle

Wanting the most out of life
Somewhat hindered by feelings
They are not clear or hidden away
They are just there in my mind
Trapped in a world of confusion
Not knowing what to say or do
Each day is another
One that may bring the truth
Until this awaited moment
For me
Living is a success of its own

Bryony Carr, June 2005

Youth Cancer Trust

Thank you for all of your
Help
And support
Not to forget the love care and
Kindness that

You gave to
Our group of eight
Understanding and full-filling each of our needs

Someone in my mind is telling me
Only very special people

May have this chance to be free
Undergoing times of hard and times of joy, but
Coming here to YCT gave me
Hope for the future

                                                      Bryony Carr, June 2005

Written for Brenda Clark and James Keating

The Youth Cancer Trust is a respite home for young people undergoing or recovering from cancer treatment. Staying here has helped me build up my confidence and form lifelong friendships.

Destiny Verses Fate

Sitting in the waiting room
Without knowledge of my future
Thoughts inside you of pure desperation
Doubting your own presence
Thinking of things that might happen
But may be halted in this journey
All this is a strange world of silence

Bryony Carr, August 2005

Not Believing

I prefer to see the sunshine
I prefer to see the glory
Not the sadness
Not taking anyone's word for it
The diagnosis of my Cancer
Not believing the truth in front of my eyes
My own feelings and no others
Thinking about life, my life
Lies and more lies
Not knowing the truth
The truth is my destiny
Words are just words
Letters are just letters
And nothing else

Bryony Carr, October 2005

Someone Invisible

An image in your mind of a person digging
Digging into the ground for a piece of hope
Someone who needs to express feelings
And show to the world
What they want to say
Rather than what has been said before
A person full of life
Needing the help and care from all who listen
Feelings shared with others
A face smiling in its happiness
Arms and legs staying strong
And the feet standing sturdy in joy

Bryony Carr, November 2005

A Spicy Breeze

The beginning
A spicy breeze present and strong
And beyond
A shadow is seen in the distance
Tall and leaning
Is this body going to fall to the ground?
No, safe from the wind
She, or he, walks along the sandy beach
The sun shines brightly behind this unknown body
Stepping over any sandcastles in the way
Built from encouragement and joy
Children laughing, squinting in the seaside glare
Sounds floating around in the air
The people and the creatures of this world are alive
The end

Bryony Carr, November 2005

A Hard Game To Play

My dream about playing tennis, table that is
I hear noises, the sounds of "ping" and "pong"
One moment of standing alone
A "ping" echoing my fall
A "pong" announcing out loud my actions
An atmosphere of fear and the unknown
Heavy breathing and a mouth spluttering strange words
Hitting these back against the barrier between life and death

Bryony Carr, January 2006

Breaking Free

The dark sky
Doesn't ever get lighter
A few stars are shining far far away
The window is between my
Life inside the and outside
In the real world
I know that someday I will flee from here

Bryony Carr, February 2006

Darkness

Alone in the dark
With nothing to say or do
Except stare into space
And wonder about things
Special things
Lonely
No one can help
Please understand
For I know that you can
Sometimes my life is hard
And other times it can be great
But I have to realise
That this is all to do with
Growing up
A vital part of living
Who knows what lies ahead
Of blackened lives
For me, I hope to live
Unsure as I am
I need to be alive
Please

Bryony Carr, February 2006

Tracy Ann House

Young cancer patients
Can spend time in Bournemouth
Tracy Ann House welcomes you

The opportunity to
Relax and rest
Away from home
Can you do anything? (A question often asked)
Yes, options galore!

Activities range from horse riding, bowling to watching films
Near to the beach, walk in the sand, swim in the sea
Next door is a hotel, Riviera

Here you can swim and play in the indoor and
Outdoor swimming pool and ample
Use of the
Sauna and jacuzzi
Everything at YCT is a gift, something to remember

Bryony Carr, March, 2006

Tracy Ann House is a respite home run by Brenda Clark and James Keating. It is named after Brenda's daughter, who died from cancer.

Being Invisible

I've seen a face
One which I remember looking lost and confused
Thinking of what might have been
Before the beginning of this dream
Some hope can be born and held as a picture of reality
A voice, soft and gentle, echoes in the distant past
Repeating words that are known to all
A strange and concerning situation
One that is forever in my thoughts

Bryony Carr, May 2006

Slipping Away

I can't stop it
It cascades down like a waterfall
My eyes are moist
My face feels soft
And out of nowhere appears a shadow

Bryony Carr, June 2006

Yearly Curing Troubles

You can see life in the sea
Or play pool in the pool
Up high on a horse
Thriving in the New Forest
Hope lies here

Confidence and independence
Are raised up to the sky
Next to new friends, we
Can be free
Every problem we have to face just disappears
Running away from harm, I

Truly believe
Realising it's not the end but a new beginning
Underneath all and sundry, is a
Solution, a place named
The Youth Cancer Trust

Bryony Carr, July 2006

Written for Brenda Clark and James Keating

Robert Wakeham

Robert aka Rob
Or aka the little Bob Marley
Being young and fit
Everything that he did was filled with enthusiasm and fun and
Really showed that the important
Things to him were to be together with his family and friends

We were
All bound together like a bunch of grapes
Keeping positive and having faith
Each day that passed all his friends
Hoped and wanted peace
A special group of youngsters who care about others
Many will remember Rob as a jewel in the night sky

Bryony Carr, August 2006

Robert was a friend I met through a young person's support group. He sadly succumbed to his illness several years ago. I will always remember him with a big smile on his face.

Mr. Sood

Share your problems
Over the counter
Or face to face to
Decide on the right treatment

Choosing the best with friendly
Help and advice
Each and everyone may be helped for any
Minor or more serious conditions
It's on Gloucester Road, a road well-known in Bristol for its
Stylish and unique shops
The ideal place to be

Bryony Carr, October 2006

Mr. Sood is my pharmacist who sorts out all my prescriptions. His help has been invaluable over the years.

Sally Le Masurier

Sally is a wonderful nurse
Always caring and giving
Lots of help and support along with a
Lovely bedside manner
Year after year after year

Listening to the children and parents
Each and everyone

More positive but honest thoughts and answers
All in an atmosphere full of hope, she always believes in
Showing a happy and friendly face
Underneath all of her help and support, she knows and can understand the
Realistic and difficult problems that we face
In the medical world of today
Entering into a place where all questions are focused on the
Reality of life

Bryony Carr, November 2006

Sally was a nurse at the hospital where I was treated. She became a good friend and we developed a close friendship. We have stayed friends ever since.

Imagination

Sitting and waiting for the
Doors to be unlocked
I have no key to open these forbidden barriers
Somehow I am allowed to go and rest as
I have been blessed as the special one
Entering this kingdom of eternal life
My body is floating up the creek
Tests done here and there, up and down
I want an answer
A good one I hope

Bryony Carr, December 2006

Answers To Questions

There must be a reason for thinking about 'why'
Why there are times in our lives that are questioned
And why are we already created before we enter this world?
Are we alive or are we dead?
Are we female or are we male?
Are we black or are we white?
Are we young or are we old?
Are we living on planet Earth or are we living on the Moon?
Why 'oh' why 'oh' why?
Eventually life will tell

Bryony Carr, January 2007

A Boy

Seeing a young boy
Playing on his computer
Listening to music, hard rock sounds
Having no worries in his very special world
His brave vibes permeate the air
A feeling of being complete and carefree

Bryony Carr, January 2007

Normality

Being in the only place
Where things seem to be always equal
Our lives are very similar
In a way which is controlled
By humanity
We live as normal
Talking, laughing and enjoying our times together
Seeing the family and friends
This place is far away
Distant from reality
Having an atmosphere bursting full of love and joy
I can finally see and begin to
Think about our long journey into the future and beyond
All in peace and tranquillity

Bryony Carr, January 2007

Hanging On

Sitting and waiting
For the doors to be unlocked
My life is a mess
Tests here, there and everywhere
A well-known place I can do without
I need an answer
A good one I hope

Bryony Carr, March 2007

Four Become Two

A thought of being utterly blessed in this world
Yet in the back of the mind
There will always be questions about your own mortality
And knowing the ultimate truth about life
Strange and mystic feelings
Atmospheres being very quiet and calm
All with the ancient belief of staying complete and content
There must be a clear and positive way to freedom

Bryony Carr, March 2007

Religion and Signals

A very strange and mystic feeling
The atmosphere being quiet and cold
An ancient belief of peace to all mankind
There must be a way forward

Bryony Carr, May 2007

My Love For Your Life

There is something that I need to say
How I miss you everyday
I think about the times we spent together
And I know we will be friends forever
Please do not be sad that we had to part
I feel I have lost a piece of my heart
This space will always be reserved for you
And only you can fit into this special place
Maybe in the future we can join up again
And together we can fly up high in the sky

Bryony Carr, July 2007

An Ode To Love

What can I say about the lady with the biggest heart
So many things I don't know where to start
I met you last year, so thoughtful and kind
The nicest person I could hope to find
You're friendly, funny and talkative too
I'm looking forward to September and seeing you

Paul Kearsley, July 2007

Jamie's Death

One thing I like to think
Is that the people we love
Have never really left us
But are always looking out for us

                                    Beverley East-Watson, July 2007

I Do

Do I walk?
Do I talk?
Do I fall off a wall?
Do I live?
Do I die and fly up to the sky?
Does the world cry?
Do I pray?
Do I know my way?
Do I need you to be near?
Am I in fear?
Do I shed a tear?
Do I want peace?
I do know I want this pain to cease

Bryony Carr, July 2007

My Brain's Eyes

An image in my mind
Seeing strength and courage
It reminds me of a life
Once here and now gone
He comes into my thoughts
Someone precious
A life just wasted into thin air

Bryony Carr, July 2007

Jamie

To his friends he was known as Buddha
To his family he was just our Jamie
He never gave up
He never complained
He was strong for us
And that's how it remained
We all loved that boy very much
To everybody's heart he touched
Every week without fail Jamie would come around to eat his Sunday roast
He always said he loves his grandma the most
We will never forget the beautiful boy
He will be walking with angels, tall and strong
He will be telling them all how to get along
He was tall
He was young
He was my beautiful grandson

Winifred Terry, July 2007

It's Heaven and My Haven

Floating around and around
Inside a bubble of hope
All of us together in a
Blind mist of almost nothing
Remembering the sayings
Of our peers
Shouting and then slowly
The whispers heard in the distance
They look up to us in our special place
In this world and leave us in peace
The world containing our lives

Bryony Carr, September 2007

Detached

All alone in the darkness
With distant dreams of being by myself
Playing solitaire in the middle of nowhere
Not a sound to be heard
Doing everything on my territory
Sorting out and dealing with troubles that occur endlessly
Keeping sane throughout
Always being sensible but
In the back of my mind
Always trying to understand why this uphill journey
Has been sent to me
Testing my ability to survive during this time of my life

Bryony Carr, October 2007

A Beautiful Portrait

I see a face
One which I adore
Thoughts of what may have been
Before the note
Words reaching out saying now it's the end
Hope and belief has been born
Held up and shown as a picture
Right in front of our eyes
Hanging around for
A day, a week, a month, a year?
Not even to be questioned
Never to be removed from the lives living in this everlasting world
This image is loved by all
It's here to stay until eternity

Bryony Carr, December 2007

In The Mirror

Bryony, is it me?
Reflecting the bright colours of a flower, it's too
Young to fade away, a fence is in the distance, a hurdle is in
  the way, a thought
On my mind, do I jump or bump or live or die?
Now, do I fall or stand tall in this troubled
Year of my life?

Cancer will not win and send me into
An early grave, I am
Ready to be strong and
Rescue myself from harm

Can Cancer Be Just A Word?

Bryony Carr, February 2008

Words That Speak

I say, no response, nothing
An image of voices and sounds that are said but not heard
The quietness is noted
Then in a moment of shock
These invisible words are shouted out loud
And have a reason to be stated to all that listen
Important things are not often understood
Letters, words, sentences, paragraphs
Turned around and around into pages of reality
Creating a tale including these silent words
In the end a story is born
Revealing mass confusion to those who attempt to read

Bryony Carr, March 2008

20 Special Songs

1. Three Little Birds, Bob Marley, 1977
2. I Can See Clearly Now, Johnny Nash, 1972
3. She's Like The Wind, Patrick Swayze, 1987
4. Watermark, Enya, 1988
5. Eternal Flame, Bangles, 1989
6. Sacrifice, Elton John, 1989
7. From A Distance, Bette Midler, 1990
8. Save The Best For Last, Vanessa Williams, 1991
9. Chi Mai, Ennio Morricone, 1987
10. The Final Countdown, Europe, 1986
11. Born To Try, Delta Goodrem, 2002
12. Babe, Take That, 1993
13. I Believe I Can Fly, R. Kelly, 1996
14. The Power Of Love, Jennifer Rush, 1985
15. Stay Another Day, East 17, 1995
16. The Heart Takes Pleasure First, Michael Nyman, 1995
17. Earth Song, Michael Jackson, 1995
18. Fields Of Gold, Eva Cassidy, 1996
19. A Different Beat, Boyzone, 1998
20. 7 Seconds, Neneh Cherry & Youssou N'Dour, 2004

Some of these songs remind me of the people who have made a big difference to my life:

1. Jamie D. Buckfield, friend
2. Derek J. Carr, father
4. Lorna W. Howard, grandmother
5. Jill F. Carr, mother
9. Stephen P. Lowis, oncologist
11. Alexander D. Simms, friend
13. Erica J. Carr, sister
16. Sylvia J. Frost, piano teacher
17. Sally A. Le Masurier, friend
18. Emma M. Weeks, friend
20. Susannah Knowles, friend

Bryony Carr, March 2008

Tainted Love

Who can explain what love is?
I believe that love is a disease
A harsh disorder that affects many minds
Love is infectious
All our deep feelings can settle down to rest and stay forever
An important reason to show these messages of hope to all that listen
Love is treatable if we let these emotions be cured
But healing reality doesn't work for most
These thoughts stay inside the heart
Embedded inside the walls of treasure
A distant voice states that love should never be removed
Overtime the love we hold close to our hearts
Spreads throughout the body

Bryony Carr, April 2008

30, Young or Old ?

30 days in the month before May
30 days has September, April, June and November
30 pence was my pocket money when I was young and free
30 exams to pass in my science degree
30 minutes in half an hour
30 seconds in half a minute
30 is seen by the eye as two single numbers joined together to be a three and a nought
30 degrees Centigrade is 86 degrees Fahrenheit
30 red roses, a gift from a special friend
30 is trente in the French language
30 is **XXX** in Latin
30 is λ in Greek
30 years in the life of Bryony Carr
30 divided by three and adding two = 12 years of my journey through cancer; full of light and dark memories
30 years of age was once a dream but now it's a miracle

Bryony Carr, May 2008

My Unwanted Dream

Moving into the circle of life
Exploring where to thrive and expand its wings
Drifting into the unknown
Unfamiliar with the surroundings
Leaving behind the unborn
Like a swallow flying into a flock of birds
Once an individual, now in an army
Being all together and having the power to strike
Leading the way to fight for independence
And invade the chosen body
Showing their presence here in this new place
To look and see any danger that may cause disruption
Other questions need to be asked
Most are "why?"
Answers can be found on the wall of my life

Bryony Carr, June 2008

Brenda, Jim and Georgie

Blooming like a rose
Resembling the Queen of Hearts
Every breath she takes is filled with love
Never forgetting the warmth of her smile
Deflecting an image of
A lady with a beautiful soul

Jim, a nickname of the King of Hearts
A gentleman made of gold
Maybe a diamond in disguise
Eager to help and support those in need
Showing all his love for life

Giving all that she can
Easy going and efficient in her ways
Optimistic day after day
Ready to give the
Gift of life, help and support to all
If anyone asks a favour, yes is always the answer
Noble in her ambitions
A high spirited woman

Bryony Carr, October 2008

Brenda, Jim and Georgina are true friends of mine who do a wonderful job at the Youth Cancer Trust in Bournemouth.

Numbers

One and Two – I love you
Three and Four – le Bryony j'adore
Five and Six – Without you I'm in a fix
Seven and Eight – I cannot wait
Nine and Ten – To see you again

Paul Kearsley, November 2008

A Perfect Day

A girl playing with her doll
A boy watching his favourite cartoon
A teenager playing his guitar
A teenager learning to drive
A father going to work
A mother cooking dinner
A perfect day in an ideal world
A place in this scene is always free
Open to those who wish to have this chance
My three J's are flying into this circle of life
But after time one loving soul disappears
Fluttering higher into the sky above our world
Leaving two friends with memories and strength forever
My three J's will always be standing high in front of my eyes

Bryony Carr, January 2009

A Lady With A True Smile

Wind in the summer sun
A figure is seen in the distance
A beautiful portrait of a woman
She is walking in the sand
Along the beach
Stepping over sandcastles built by the children here in our world
The sun is shining down from above
Seagulls are flying high in the sky
A prayer is uttered by the sea
Amen

Bryony Carr, May 2009

Written for my late grandmother, Lorna Howard

Rhyme Verses Time

The sea is walking along the waves
The sun is talking down to its rays
The wind is singing loudly
The rain is pouring down proudly
A way of thinking
A scary thought of sinking
A line can split
A piece of a jigsaw doesn't fit
An arm turns into a leg
A child is scared
The crying never stops
Not just the young
Not just the old
A dove flies overhead
Peace is spread
Feelings are said
A world has light in its sight

Bryony Carr, June 2009

Living Three Lives

A life before Cancer
A life with Cancer
A life after Cancer

A historical story

                                  Bryony Carr, August 2009